A
Literature Unit
for

The Big Wave

by Pearl S. Buck

Written by Susan Onion

Teacher Created Materials, Inc.
P.O. Box 1040
Huntington Beach, CA 92647
©1998 Teacher Created Materials, Inc.
Made in U.S.A.

ISBN 1-55737-616-X

Illustrated by
Phil Hopkins

Edited by
Randi E. Suppe, M.S. Ed.

Cover Art by
Wendy Chang

Table of Contents

- Quiz Time
- Hands-On Project: Counting in Japanese
- Cooperative Learning Activity: Living Words
- Curriculum Connection: Volcanoes
- Into Your Life: Family Trip

- Quiz Time
- Hands-On Project: Paint the Ocean
- Cooperative Learning Activity: What Is a Big Wave?
- Curriculum Connection: Earthquake Preparation
- Into Your Life: Warning Signals

- Quiz Time
- Hands-On Project: Memories
- Cooperative Learning Activity: Words of Wisdom
- Curriculum Connection: Different Foods
- Into Your Life: Traditions

- Quiz Time
- Hands-On Project: Beautiful Scrolls
- Cooperative Learning Activity: Rich or Poor?
- Curriculum Connection: Haiku
- Into Your Life: Miniature Garden

- Quiz Time
- Hands-On Project: Three-Dimensional Map
- Cooperative Learning Activity: Fear
- Curriculum Connection: Japan Map
- Into Your Life: Changes Around Town

Introduction

A good book can touch our lives like a good friend. Within its pages are words and characters that can inspire us to achieve our highest ideals. We can turn to it for companionship, recreation, comfort, and guidance. It also gives us a cherished story to hold in our hearts forever.

In Literature Units, great care has been taken to select books that are sure to become good friends!

Teachers who use this unit will find the following features to supplement their own valuable ideas:

- A Sample Lesson Plan
- Pre-reading Activities
- A Bibliographical Sketch and Picture of the Author
- A Book Summary
- Vocabulary Lists and Vocabulary Activity Ideas
- Chapters grouped for study, with each section including the following:
  - a quiz
  - a hands-on project
  - a cooperative learning activity
  - a cross-curriculum connection
  - an extension into the reader's own life
- Post-reading Activities:
  - book report ideas
  - research ideas
- A Culminating Activity
- Three Different Options for Unit Tests
- A Bibliography of Related Reading
- An Answer Key

Sample Lesson Plan

This book divides *The Big Wave* into five lesson sections. Each section has five activities and an accompanying vocabulary list. Below is a sample lesson sequence. Each lesson can take from one to several days to complete.

Lesson 1
- Introduce and discuss some or all of the pre-reading activities found on page 5.
- Read "About the Author" with your students. (page 6)

Lesson 2
- Introduce the vocabulary list for section 1. (page 8)
- Read pages 1–17. As you read, find the vocabulary words in the context of the story.
- Choose a vocabulary activity. (page 9)
- Discuss counting in Japanese. Make counting books. (page 12)
- Learn about personification. (page 13)
- Discuss and research volcanoes. (page 14)
- Compare family trips. (page 15)
- Begin Reading Reponse Journals. (page 10)
- Administer the Section 1 quiz. (page 11)

Lesson 3
- Introduce the vocabulary for section 2. (page 8)
- Read pages 18–24. As you read, find the vocabulary words in the context of the story.
- Choose a vocabulary activity. (page 9)
- Explore water and paint. (page 17)
- Learn about waves with a partner. (page 18)
- Discuss earthquake preparation and run a practice drill. (page 19)
- Design a warning system for your town. (page 20)
- Administer the Section 2 quiz. (page 16)

Lesson 4
- Introduce the vocabulary list for section 3. (page 8)
- Read pages 25–33. As you read, find the vocabulary words in the context of the story.
- Choose a vocabulary activity. (page 9)
- Make your own time capsule. (page 22)
- Work with a team to discuss words of wisdom. (page 23)
- Compare your meals with Kino's and make a Japanese soup. (page 24)

- Discuss and share family traditions. (page 25)
- Administer the Section 3 quiz. (page 21)

Lesson 5
- Introduce the vocabulary list for section 4. (page 8)
- Read pages 34–46. As you read, find the vocabulary words in the context of the story.
- Choose a vocabulary activity. (page 9)
- Make classroom scrolls. (page 27)
- Compare and contrast the rich and poor life. (page 28)
- Write haiku. (page 29)
- Create miniature gardens. (page 30)
- Administer the Section 4 quiz. (page 26)

Lesson 6
- Introduce the vocabulary list for section 5. (page 8)
- Read pages 47–57. As you read, find the vocabulary words in the context of the story.
- Choose a vocabulary activity. (page 9)
- Make a three-dimensional map of Japan. (page 32)
- Analyze characters' fears. (page 33)
- Learn about the islands that make up Japan. (page 34)
- Research the changes that have occurred in your town. (page 35)
- Administer the Section 5 quiz. (page 31)

Lesson 7
- Assign book and/or research reports. (page 36 and 37)
- Begin organizing the culminating activity. (pages 38–42)

Lesson 8
- Review the book using the polar opposites activity on page 45.
- Administer the unit test(s) of choice. (pages 43–45)
- Discuss the test answers.
- Discuss students' enjoyment of the book.
- Provide a list of related reading for your students. (page 46)

Before the Book

Before you begin reading *The Big Wave* with your students, do some pre-reading activities to stimulate interest and to enhance reading comprehension. Here are some activities that might work well in your class.

1. Predict what the story might be about by hearing the title and looking at the cover.

2. Ask your students if any of them have read any other novel written by Pearl S. Buck.

3. Discuss the Pulitzer and Nobel Prizes awarded for adult literature. (Pearl S. Buck won both of these.) You might want to discuss the Caldecott awards for best picture book and the Newbery awards given for the best children's literature.

4. Build upon students' prior knowledge by discussing Japan, the Pacific Ocean, volcanoes, fishing, farming, traditions, friendship, and tsunamis.

5. Discuss and answer these questions:

   Would you ever…

   …choose to be poor if it meant being with people you care about?

   …invite your best friend to live with you?

   …live near a volcano?

   …swim to an island?

   …choose the same career as your parents?

   Have you ever…

   …experienced an earthquake or been near an active volcano?

   …had to move away from a place or people you liked?

6. Locate Japan and the surrounding Pacific Islands on a map. Have students research the ring of fire which circles the Pacific. Share this information with the class. Ask students to imagine what it would be like to live on one of these volcanic islands.

About the Author

Pearl S. Buck was born in Hillsboro, West Virginia, on July 26, 1892. Soon after she was born, her family decided to return to China where her father and mother worked as Presbyterian missionaries. As a child in China, she learned to speak Chinese and use chopsticks, and she dressed in traditional Chinese clothes. She said that she always preferred to eat Chinese foods.

China was a volatile region during this time in history. When Pearl S. Buck was only four years old, the Boxer Rebellion took place, and her family was forced to flee for safety. Two years later the family returned home, but their home never felt the same.

As a teenager, Pearl S. Buck attended a boarding school in Shanghai. Upon graduation she returned to the United States to go to school at Randolph-Macon College in Virginia. During this time, she tried to learn what it was like to be an American.

Pearl S. Buck always felt that she was straddling the two different cultures of China and the United States. She spent the next several years teaching English literature at universities in both China and the United States. She also began writing at this time.

In 1932 Pearl S. Buck was awarded the Pulitzer Prize for her novel *The Good Earth*. She continued writing, often working on more than one book at a time. In 1938 she was the first woman to receive the Nobel Prize for Literature. During the following years, Pearl S. Buck received many other awards and honors for her writing.

In later years, Pearl S. Buck became very active in child welfare work. She adopted five children and founded The Welcome House, Inc. This agency helped secure the adoptions of Asian-American children. In 1964, she also established the Pearl S. Buck Foundation to help Asian-American children born in Asia. She always felt that it was important for children to live with families.

Pearl S. Buck enjoyed music, children, people, and books. Her family was very important to her. She died at the age of 80 in Vermont. During her life, she had written more than 85 books, many of which have been translated into other languages. Several of her novels have also been adapted for movie and audio productions.

The Big Wave

by Pearl S. Buck

(HarperCollins Children's Books, 1986)

(Available in Canada and UK from HarperCollins Publishers Ltd; Australia, HarperCollins)

Kino and Jiya are two boys who live on the coast of Japan. Although they are best friends, they have very different lives. Kino's family lives on a farm on the hillside. The family members work hard planting and harvesting crops on the fields that were terraced by their ancestors centuries ago. Jiya's family lives in the fishing village on the beach at the base of the mountain. Jiya helps his father on the fishing boat when he goes out to sea. During the winter season the boys attend school in the village, and after school and work they often play and swim in the ocean together. Life is good, yet both families realize that they live in danger being situated between a great volcano and the ocean.

One day the great volcano awakens. Everyone in the village and on the hillside stays close to home to watch the earth and the sea. As the ocean becomes calm, rich Old Gentleman urgently rings a bell, summoning the villagers to take shelter with him on the hillside behind his castle walls. The bell continues tolling as reluctant villagers leave their homes to seek shelter on higher ground. Many fishermen refuse to leave their boats and send only their wives and children to safety. Jiya's father orders Jiya to climb to safety. Instead of going to Old Gentleman's castle, Jiya decides to go to Kino and his family.

As Jiya reaches the farm, there is a deafening roar from the sea. A huge wall of water rises from the ocean and rushes to shore. Water reaches the beach before anyone in the village can be warned. The wave quickly recedes and sweeps the entire village out to sea, leaving nothing behind on the sand. The village and villagers are gone. Jiya faints and Kino and his father carry him to their home.

When Jiya finally awakens from his shock and realizes that he is an orphan, Kino and his family welcome him as a new member into their home. Old Gentleman has also taken an interest in Jiya and offers to make Jiya his rich son. After visiting the castle and talking with Old Gentleman, Jiya chooses to live with Kino's family where he knows he will be loved.

Jiya grows up and learns the trade of farming, but he is not happy. He longs for the sea. He decides to save his money to buy a boat. Before moving back to the fishing village to his new house, he takes Kino's sister as his wife. Together they start their lives with a new respect for the sea.

Vocabulary Lists

On this page are vocabulary lists which correspond to each sectional grouping of pages. Vocabulary activity ideas can be found on page nine of this book.

SECTION 1
Pages 1–17

terraced	lacquered
ancestors	wiry
thatched	corded
cobbled	sheaves
knoll	threshed
gratitude	haste
phosphorescent	reap
fragrant	zenith

SECTION 2
Pages 18–24

tolled	ebbing
limp	subsiding
urgently	sorrowfully
frothing	

SECTION 3
Pages 25–33

renewing	pleasant
horizon	tenderly
fetch	threshold
faltered	sorrow
snatching	midst
broth	

SECTION 4
Pages 34–46

sturdily	benefits
province	determined
propose	ancient
persuade	exquisite
stern	hearth

SECTION 5
Pages 47–57

booty

musing

mildly

refuge

furrow

mischievous

Vocabulary Activity Ideas

You can help your students learn and retain the vocabulary in *The Big Wave* by providing them with interesting vocabulary activities. Here are a few ideas to try.

❏ **True or False Definitions** — This game should be played before students have looked up or have become familiar with a new list of words. The goal of this game is to guess which students are presenting the correct definition. Make up three definition cards for each vocabulary word. One of these cards should have the correct definition. Be sure to mark this card as special. Select three students to be on the definition preparation panel and hand each student on the panel a definition card. Write the new vocabulary word on the board for the class to see. The students on the panel take turns reading their definition cards to the class. The student with the true definition must read the card as written. The students who hold the unmarked made-up definitions may make up other fictional definitions if they choose. The remaining students in the class then vote to see which is the true definition. Points may be earned for correct guesses. Rotate students so all students have a chance to be on the panel.

❏ **Group Short Stories** — Divide your class into groups and then ask the groups to create short stories which include all of the vocabulary words assigned. See which team can make up the shortest, funniest, or most exciting story.

❏ **Vocabulary Bingo** — Hand out blank bingo grids to students. Have them place one vocabulary word in each space on the sheet. Students may place the words in any order on the sheet. Then randomly choose and read the vocabulary definitions. A student wins by covering a row or column of words as the definitions are read.

❏ **Pictionary** — Students take turns drawing pictures that illustrate the vocabulary words while the rest of the class tries to guess which word is being illustrated.

❏ **One-sentence Challenge** — Challenge your students to create one sentence using as many vocabulary words as possible. Be sure that the sentences make sense!

❏ **Vocabulary Charades** — Have students act out vocabulary words while the rest of the class attempts to guess which words are being portrayed.

❏ **Team Presentations** — Divide the class into teams and assign each team groups of words to present to the rest of the class. Teams are responsible for looking up the assigned words and for designing a presentation which will help everyone to remember the meanings. Teams may use dramatics, drawings, songs, rhymes, or any other creative approach in their presentations.

❏ **Puzzles** — Have students create crossword puzzles or word searches using some of the vocabulary words from their word lists.

Reading Response Journals

One great way to ensure that the reading of *The Big Wave* touches each student in a personal way is to include the use of reading response journals in your plans. Ask students to create a journal for *The Big Wave*. Assemble journals using a method and materials that suit your classroom needs. In these journals, students can be encouraged to respond to the story in a number of ways. Here are a few ideas.

- Tell students that the purpose of the journal is to record their thoughts, ideas, observations, and questions as they read *The Big Wave*.

- Provide students with, or ask them to suggest, topics from the story that would stimulate writing. Here is an example that might be drawn from the first few pages of the story.

  —Although Kino feels the sea is beautiful, his friend Jiya considers it an enemy. There is often both danger and beauty in nature. Think about one of the forces of nature and how a person may see it as a threat or a thing of beauty. Write a brief description of the force of nature from both points of view.

- After reading each chapter, students can write about what they learned in the chapter.

- Ask students to draw their responses to certain events or characters in the story, using the blank pages in their journals.

- Tell students that they may use their journals to record diary-type responses that they may want to enter.

- Encourage students to bring their journal ideas to life! Ideas generated from their journal writing can be used to create plays, debates, stories, songs, and art displays.

- Allow students time to write in their journals daily. To evaluate the journals, you may wish to use the following guidelines:

  —Personal reflections will be read by the teacher, but no corrections will be made or letter grades assigned. Credit is given for effort, and all students who sincerely try will be awarded credit. If a grade is desired for this type of entry, grade according to the number of journal entries completed. For example, if five journal assignments were made and the student conscientiously completes all five, then he or she should receive an "A."

  —Nonjudgmental teacher responses should be made as you read the journals to let the students know that you are reading and enjoying their journals. Here are some types of responses that will please your journal writers and encourage them to write more.

    "You have really found what's important in the story!"

    "You've made me feel as if I were there."

    "If you feel comfortable, I'd like you to share this with the class. I think they will enjoy it as much as I have."

Quiz Time

1. List three major events which take place in this section of the story.

   _____

   _____

   _____

2. Describe the fields around Kino's farm. How are they different from most farms that you know?

   _____

   _____

3. Where do Jiya and the other fisherfolk live?

   _____

4. How does Jiya explain that his house does not have a window facing the sea?

   _____

   _____

5. Who lives in the castle on the knoll?

   _____

6. What do Kino and Jiya do when they swim to Deer Island?

   _____

7. What does Jiya worry about while he is on the island?

   _____

   _____

8. Where did Kino and his family go on holiday last fall?

   _____

9. Why is Kino glad that his father is a farmer and not a fisherman?

   _____

   _____

10. Why does Kino's father say that he will not sleep?

   _____

Counting in Japanese

Kino and Jiya both attend school during the winter months. There they learn to read, write, and do math. It is hard work, but the boys enjoy it. Learning to read and write the Japanese language is not easy. The Japanese system for writing words and numbers is different from English. Words are especially difficult. Instead of using an alphabet of twenty-six letters, the Japanese use many different symbols. Often the symbol stands for a whole word. There are thousands of symbols to learn in the Japanese language.

Use the chart below to practice saying and writing the numbers one through ten in Japanese. Then work with a partner to make your own Japanese counting book to share with the class.

Number	Japanese Symbol	Japanese Pronunciation
1	一	ee-chee
2	二	nee
3	三	sahn
4	四	shee
5	五	go
6	六	ro-koo
7	七	shee-chee
8	八	hah-chee
9	九	koo
10	十	joo

Challenge: Try writing some word problems using the Japanese number symbols. Exchange with a friend to see if you can solve the problems.

Living Words

When Jiya is talking about his fear of the ocean, he says that he is watching to see if the ocean is angry. Since the ocean is not alive, it cannot have feelings and, therefore, cannot really be angry. But if we close our eyes, an angry ocean is easy to imagine. We call this personification. Another example of personification is a crying cloud. Sometimes a writer describes a noun by giving it human qualities, such as anger or sorrow, to help us better understand the image and to make the writing more interesting.

Personifying objects can be a lot of fun. Sometimes we can create silly images just by mixing and combining words. Below is a list of nouns and a list of human qualities. Work with a partner to write your own personifications for the nouns. Then think of some nouns to match with the list of human qualities. Remember that your goal is to create an image that is easy for your reader to see because it has familiar human qualities.

After you have finished, choose at least five of your personifications and use them in a story. Personifications will make your writing more interesting and lively.

Nouns	Human Qualities
wind	
shoe	
pencil	
umbrella	
rain	
pig	
paper	
	laughing
	smiling
	happy
	nervous
	sweating
	naughty
	crying

Volcanoes

What is a volcano?

A volcano is formed when hot molten rock, called magma, is forced up through the crust of the earth. As the volcano erupts, sometimes ash and toxic gases also explode through the crust, creating an opening, or vent, in the top or sides of the volcano's cone. Volcanoes usually take one of two forms. They either occur as a long crack in the surface, or they take the shape of a large cone.

When the magma flows from the volcano onto the surface, we call it lava. It is the cooling lava and the settling ash that form the cone shape around the base of the volcano. The opening or hole is called a vent. Sometimes volcanoes form more than one vent as the pressure builds up inside the cone.

Where do volcanoes come from?

There are four different layers of material inside the earth. The thin outer layer is the crust. This is made up of slabs of rock. The next layer is the mantle. The mantle is very thick and is made of hot, liquid rock. This rock reaches temperatures of over 1,000 degrees Celsius (1832° F)! Finally, there are the outer core, which is liquid metal, and the inner core, which is solid iron. The magma which forces its way to the surface when a volcano erupts comes from the upper portion of the mantle. This is the magma chamber.

Use the information above to help you label these diagrams. Then work with a partner to find out more about the eruptions of these volcanoes: Mt. St. Helens, Vesuvius, Krakatoa, Mt. Pelée.

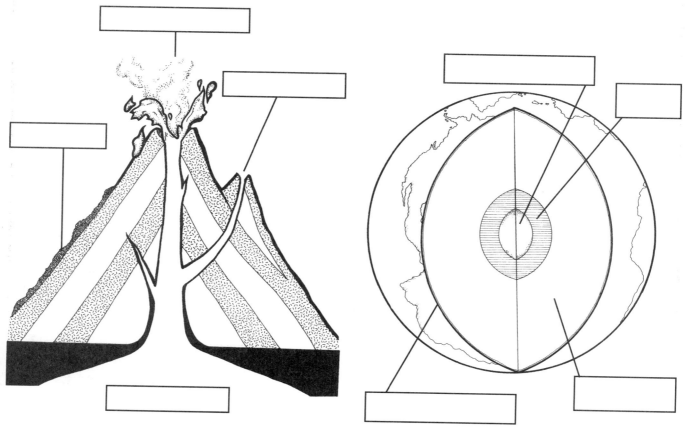

Family Trip

Every autumn Kino and his family went on a family trip. Kino remembers that during their last family trip they traveled to a famous volcano twenty miles away.

Many families take trips together. Sometimes they visit other family members on holidays, or they travel to new and exciting places. Taking family trips is a great way to learn about new places and to meet new people. Think about a trip that you have taken with your family. Use the back of this paper to answer the following questions.

- **Where did you travel with your family?**
- **How did you get there?**
- **Had anyone in your family ever visited this place before?**
- **What new things did you see or learn about on your trip?**
- **Would you like to travel to this place again? Why or why not?**
- **Where would you like to go on your next family trip? Why?**

In the space below, make a map plotting where you started your trip and where you ended. Note any towns or states that you passed through. Also show any landmarks, such as bridges or lakes, that you saw. Include a key to explain any symbols that you use on your map.

Teacher Note: Post a map of the United States (or the world) in the classroom and have each student put a pin, with his or her name attached, on the place where he or she traveled. If some of your students traveled locally, also place a regional map on display.

Quiz Time

1. List three major events which take place in this section of the story.

   _____

   _____

   _____

2. Why does Old Gentleman raise a flag and ring a bell?

   _____

   _____

3. What would you do if you lived in the fishing village and heard the bell?

   _____

   _____

4. What do you think happened when Kino's father saw the flag and heard the bell twice before?

   _____

   _____

5. Why does Jiya's father send Jiya up the mountainside to safety?

   _____

   _____

6. Does Jiya go to the castle? Why or why not?

   _____

7. What happens to the fishing village?

   _____

8. What does Jiya do after he sees the big wave?

   _____

9. Why do you think Kino's father let Kino keep crying?

   _____

10. What does Kino's father decide to do after Jiya loses his family?

   _____

Paint the Ocean

In the story *The Big Wave*, Pearl S. Buck uses many color words to describe how the ocean appears. She describes the ocean before the storm as a silvery blue-green. During the storm it is purple-gray. After the storm the ocean is a calm sparkling blue.

Skim through the story to find as many words as you can that describe the ocean. Each time you find a description, close your eyes and try to imagine what the ocean would look like.

You can explore the watery, rich colors of the ocean and create your own beautiful work of art by combining paint and water.

Materials:

- paper
- flat pan
- oil paint
- sticks (Paint sticks work well.)
- cold water
- old shirt or smock

Directions:

1. Fill the pan with cold water.

2. Select paint colors that you would find in the ocean. Use a stick to drip some paint onto the top of the water. (Choose at least two different ocean colors for your painting.) Use the tip of a stick to swirl the paint so the color is spread over the surface of the water.

3. Gently lay a sheet of paper on the surface of the water. Allow the paper to rest for about 10 seconds.

4. Lift the paper out of the water and set it aside to dry.

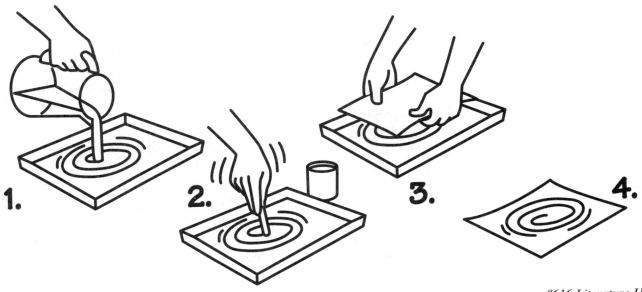

What Is a Big Wave?

A tsunami is a huge ocean wave caused by an earthquake under the sea. When a tsunami forms it is often only a small wave a few feet high and is in the middle of the ocean. At this point, it does not look very dangerous, but as the wave travels, it picks up speed and can move up to 500 mph (800 kmph) across the ocean surface. When it reaches the shore, the bottom of the wave meets the shoreline and quickly rises. The water can rise up to 50 feet (15 m) or more in a matter of seconds! As the wave crashes on the shore, it can be very destructive.

You can learn more about waves by working with a partner to complete the following experiments.

Experiment A

Materials:

- 10-foot (3 m) length of rope.

Directions:

Stand about eight feet (2.4 m) away from your partner with each of you holding an end of the rope. One partner should hold the rope steady while the second partner slowly moves his or her end of the rope up and down to make a wave. The high part of the wave is called the crest, and the low part is called the trough. Try changing the wave by moving the rope higher and lower. What happens when you move the rope end slower or faster? Take two steps toward your partner. What happens to the waves now? What kind of waves do you think would be the most harmful in the ocean? Why?

Experiment B

Materials:

- fish tank
- water
- sand
- wooden block (long enough to fit within the inside width of the tank)
- ruler

Directions:

Pour the sand into one end of the tank and then fill the tank with water until you have a small beach. Tape the ruler to the outside of the tank at the beach end of the tank. Hold the wood block in the water at the end of the tank away from the beach and gently move it up and down to make small waves that rise about one inch (2.5 cm). What happens to the sand on the beach? Move the wood block more quickly so that the waves increase to three inches (8 cm). What happens to the sand now? Does the speed of the waves make any difference?

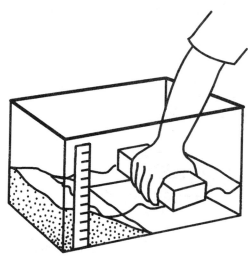

Think: If you live near the ocean or by a small pond, you can watch the impact of the waves on an actual shoreline. What changes happen as a result of the pounding water on the land?

Earthquake Preparation

When the volcano begins to erupt, Kino's family prepares for an earthquake. Kino's mother takes all of the fragile items down from the walls and packs her good dishes in straw. Kino's father remains awake at night to watch the earth and sky for changes.

In areas where earthquakes are common, schools often hold practice earthquake drills so students will know what to do in case of an emergency. Your school may already have an earthquake emergency plan in effect.

Read the earthquake drill information outlined below. Then run your own classroom earthquake drill. (If your school has its own earthquake emergency plan, you will probably want to review that drill.)

As with a fire drill, an earthquake drill also uses an alarm system. You might want to discuss an alarm sound with your principal or have your teacher blow a series of whistle blasts to signal the drill.

If inside:

Duck, cover, and hold. This means that you should duck, take cover under the nearest desk or table, and hold onto the leg of a piece of furniture. You should then wait silently in this position until given the cue, indicating that it is safe to move. Once the cue is given, quickly and silently line up at the door and exit the room to a safe place on the playground, away from any buildings or trees.

If outside:

Drop and cover. This means you should drop to the ground and cover your head. If you are near any hazards such as trees or electrical wires, roll away. Wait and remain silent until a cue is given saying that it is safe to move. Once the cue is given, you should silently walk to a specified assembly place and line up so that you can be accounted for.

Warning Signals

As the weather became more threatening, Old Gentleman gave two warning signals to the villagers. First he flew a red flag to tell the people to be prepared for an emergency. Then he rang a bell to urge the villagers to flee to the castle for safety.

Warning signals have been used all over the world for centuries. Today the United States has a nationwide emergency signaling system. It is called the Emergency Broadcasting System, or EBS. This warning system was originally designed in 1964 to be used for communication in case of a war or other national threat. Locally, this system is also used to warn people about tornadoes, floods, blizzards, or other natural emergencies. When this warning system is activated, all television and radio networks that are carriers of the system must broadcast the same warning message. All other stations must stop their own transmissions. You may have heard the testing of this signal on your local television or radio stations.

Think about where you live. What emergencies might occur in your town? If you were to develop an emergency signal system for your town, what would it be? Who would activate it? Under what circumstances would it be used? What should the people do when they hear the signal?

Brainstorm and write your ideas in the space below. Be prepared to share your signal system with your classmates.

Quiz Time

1. List three major events which take place in this section of the story.

   _____

   _____

   _____

2. What happens to the sea and sky after the storm?

   _____

   _____

3. What does Kino's family do when Jiya wakes?

   _____

   _____

4. What does Setsu offer to give to Jiya to make him feel better?

   _____

5. Why do you think Jiya feels so tired all of the time?

   _____

   _____

6. What does Kino's father say to him again and again when Kino is upset about Jiya?

   _____

7. What does Kino do while Jiya sleeps? What would you have done if you were in Kino's place?

   _____

   _____

8. How does Kino feel after he climbs the hillside to look at the volcano?

   _____

   _____

9. Why does Kino think his family is unfortunate to live in Japan?

   _____

   _____

10. What does Kino's father say about danger?

   _____

Memories

Making a Time Capsule

After Jiya's parents and brother die in the big wave, Kino is concerned that Jiya should not forget his family. Kino's father calms Kino by saying that Jiya will carry their memory in his thoughts. He says that as long as Jiya is alive, his family will live in him.

Memories are an important part of all of our lives. We learn from events in our past, and we take pleasure in sharing memorable incidents with others. Recalling our memories keeps the past alive.

You can store some of your special memories for the future by making a time capsule. For this activity you will need a container, and you will need to gather several items. A suitable container might be a coffee can, a shoe box, or a plastic container with a lid. Make sure that the container is large enough to hold all of your items and that it is easy to seal.

You might want to include some of the following items in your time capsule:

Time Capsule

- a current family picture
- a drawing
- a sample of your handwriting
- a story that you wrote
- a cassette tape of
- yourself talking, singing, or reading
- a string measurement of your height
- a list of your favorite book, song, movie, singer, actor, game, etc.

Once you have gathered your time capsule items, place them in your container and seal it. You can decorate your container to represent the present. Be sure to write the date on the side of the container.

Save your time capsule in a safe place and wait some time before you open it. In the future you might be surprised by what you learn when you look back on your memories.

Words of Wisdom

After the big wave, Kino's father talks with Kino to help him understand what has happened. He does not give Kino a simple explanation, but instead he makes some general statements about life for Kino to think about.

Work in teams of four or five to discuss what Kino's father meant by the statements below and whether you agree or disagree with them. Before beginning, assign the following jobs to your team members. Write their names on the lines provided. Be prepared to share your team results with the class in a whole group discussion.

Team Jobs:

- recorder (to write the team members' ideas)

_____

- reporter (to report to the class)

_____

- material gatherer (to collect and organize all materials needed)

_____

- reader (to read the sentences)

_____

- director (to make sure that everyone contributes something)

_____

Statements:

Life is stronger than death. (page 30)

To live in the midst of danger is to know how good life is. (page 32)

Only when he (Jiya) dares to remember his parents will he be happy again. (page 31)

Every day is more valuable now than it was before the storm. (page 26)

Different Foods

The meals that the characters in *The Big Wave* eat are probably very different from the meals that you commonly eat at home with your family. Kino ate a bowl of hot rice soup and some bean curd with tea for breakfast. For lunch his mother packed cold rice, fish, and a radish pickle. Dinner one evening consisted of rice, chicken soup, and brown fish. Soup and rice are standard foods with almost every Japanese meal. The average person in Japan eats about 165 pounds (74 kg) of rice in a year!

What are some common foods that you eat? List your meals for one day. Then compare and contrast your meals with Kino's.

Breakfast _____

_____

Lunch _____

_____

Dinner _____

_____

Would you like to eat meals like Kino's every day? Why or why not?

You can try a popular Japanese soup by following the recipe. You might want to prepare some rice to accompany your meal.

Miso Soup

Ingredients:

- 4 cups (.9 L) dashi (Japanese fish stock)
- ¹/₂ pound (225 g) tofu
- 4 tablespoons (60 mL) miso (paste made of fermented soybeans)
- chives

Directions:

1. Cut the tofu into small ¹/₂-inch (1.3 cm) squares. Cut the chive greens into ¹/₂-inch (1.3 cm) lengths.
2. Boil the dashi in a pot.
3. Add the tofu and chives to the pot.
4. Pour a small amount of the boiled dashi into a cup and add the miso. Use a whisk to stir the miso until it is dissolved. Then pour the mixture back into the pot.
5. Serve the soup immediately. (Makes four cups /.9L)

Traditions

A *tradition* is an action, belief, or custom which a person or group of people act out over and over. Often traditions are handed down from one generation to another. An example of a family tradition might be making a special cake every year to celebrate a birthday. Traditions are very important to many Japanese families. Kino and Jiya both honored special traditions in their families.

Read the traditions listed below. For each tradition, explain why you think it has importance to the characters. Be ready to share these ideas with your classmates.

The people who lived by the sea had no windows facing the water.

No one spoke at the table until the food was served to everyone.

No one wore shoes in Kino's house.

Kino's family took a holiday every fall.

Kino's father stayed awake and watched the earth and sea when the volcano was active.

Extension:
What traditions do you have in your home? On the lines below, write down your family traditions and explain why they are important to you. Be ready to share these ideas with your classmates.

_____

_____

_____

_____

_____

Quiz Time

1. List three major events which take place in this section of the story.

   _____

   _____

   _____

2. Why does Old Gentleman want to adopt Jiya?

   _____

   _____

3. What does Old Gentleman plan to do for Jiya?

   _____

4. How does Kino feel about Old Gentleman's plan?

   _____

   _____

5. Why does Kino's father send Kino with Jiya to Old Gentleman's castle?

   _____

6. Why do you think the gardener bows and makes his voice polite when he finds out who Jiya is?

   _____

   _____

7. Describe Old Gentleman.

   _____

   _____

8. What does Jiya say when Old Gentleman asks him to be his son?

   _____

9. What would Jiya miss if he did become Old Gentleman's son?

   _____

10. Who makes Jiya happy and comfortable?

   _____

Beautiful Scrolls

When Kino and Jiya enter Old Gentleman's castle, they see beautiful scrolls hanging in each room. As they meet Old Gentleman, he is painting a new scroll to hang in his entry. Sometimes scrolls have words, like Old Gentleman's new scroll; other times they have simple brush paintings of scenes in nature.

One ancient form of Japanese ink painting is called suiboku. This technique uses only a brush, ink, and water. The paintings are produced by making single brush strokes and by varying the darkness of the ink from gray to black.

You can make your own beautiful painting in this style by following the directions below.

Materials:
- paper
- water
- paintbrush
- black watercolor paint

Preparation:
Before beginning your painting, you might want to experiment with the effects of the water and paint on the paper. Try making strokes with different amounts of water and paint on your brush. Watch to see how light and dark you can make your strokes.

Directions:
1. To create the plum tree branch, begin at the lower left-hand corner of your paper and make a single bending stroke with your brush. The stroke should narrow at the end. Begin at the bend and connect another large stroke to form a branch. These two strokes should be dark, so use a fairly dry brush with lots of paint.

2. Add some small twigs to your branch. These strokes should be short and should also taper off at the ends.

3. Lastly, add some plum flowers and blossoms. (You might want to practice making some flowers before you paint them on your branches.) A complete flower has five petals with many spiky pistils. A bud shows only a couple of petals. Use only a little paint and a wet brush to make the flowers very light on your paper. The pistils can be a little darker to offset the flowers.

Finished Plum Tree Branch

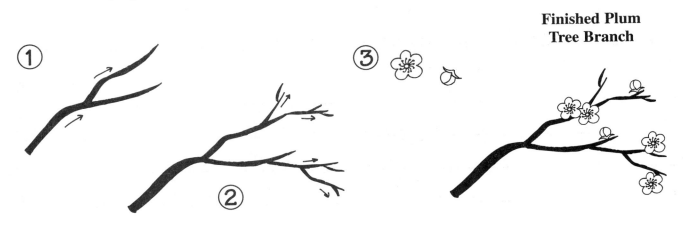

Rich or Poor?

After Jiya was orphaned, he had to make a choice about where he was going to live. He could live with wealthy Old Gentleman who would dress him in expensive clothing and send him to a fine school, or he could live with Kino's family and be a hardworking but poor farmer. This was a difficult decision for Jiya to make.

Use the Venn diagram to brainstorm. Write down images of how Jiya's life would be if he lived richly and how it would be if he lived poorly. Use the middle section to write down events that would be the same whether he were rich or poor.

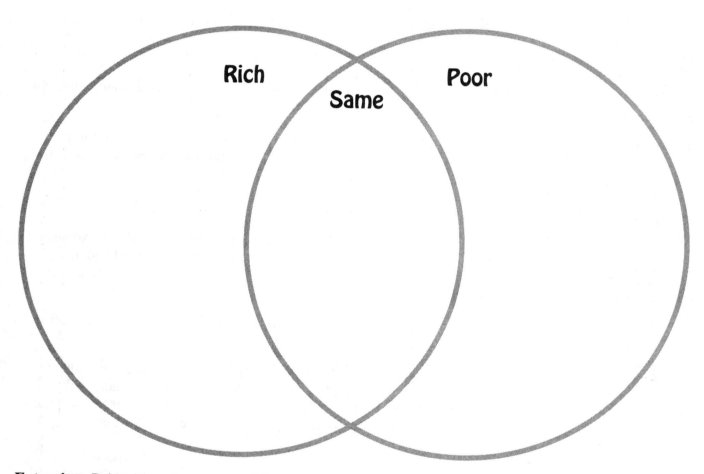

Extension: Pair with a classmate to debate whether Jiya should choose the rich life or poor life. Write some of your ideas here.

_____

_____

_____

_____

Haiku

Pearl S. Buck describes Old Gentleman's magnificent gardens when Kino and Jiya visit the castle. There is thick green moss on the ground. Pine trees, flowers, and waterfalls cover the landscape. The gardeners at Old Gentleman's castle work very hard to keep the surrounding gardens beautiful. The beauty of nature is very important in Japanese culture.

The Japanese also incorporate the richness of nature into their writing. Haiku is a Japanese style of poetry which uses the images of nature to awaken emotions. Poets have used haiku for centuries to express the beauty of seasonal changes.

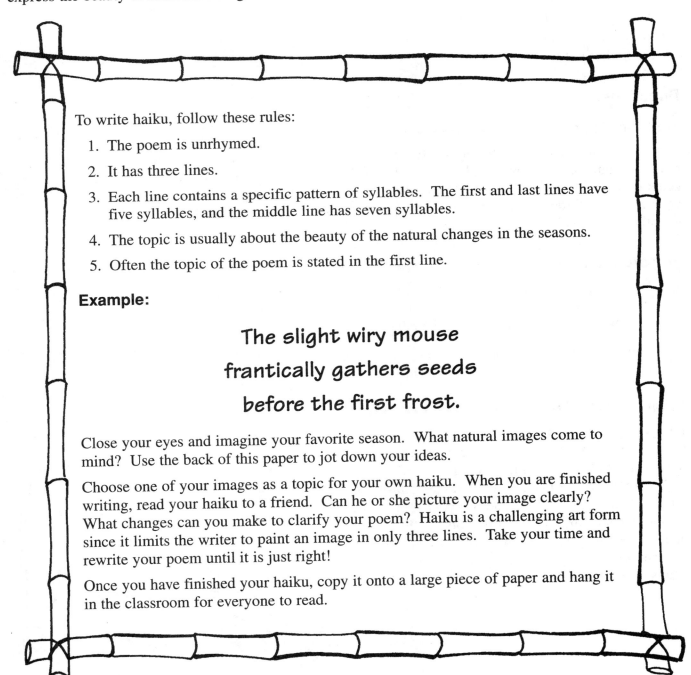

To write haiku, follow these rules:

1. The poem is unrhymed.

2. It has three lines.

3. Each line contains a specific pattern of syllables. The first and last lines have five syllables, and the middle line has seven syllables.

4. The topic is usually about the beauty of the natural changes in the seasons.

5. Often the topic of the poem is stated in the first line.

Example:

> The slight wiry mouse
>
> frantically gathers seeds
>
> before the first frost.

Close your eyes and imagine your favorite season. What natural images come to mind? Use the back of this paper to jot down your ideas.

Choose one of your images as a topic for your own haiku. When you are finished writing, read your haiku to a friend. Can he or she picture your image clearly? What changes can you make to clarify your poem? Haiku is a challenging art form since it limits the writer to paint an image in only three lines. Take your time and rewrite your poem until it is just right!

Once you have finished your haiku, copy it onto a large piece of paper and hang it in the classroom for everyone to read.

Miniature Garden

Traditionally, gardens have been very important to Japanese culture. In *The Big Wave*, Old Gentleman has beautiful gardens surrounding his castle. Many Japanese people today take great pride in creating beauty by nurturing gardens around their homes. Since garden space is limited in Japan, creating gardens in small places has become an art form. Designing a small garden can be fun. You can create your own miniature garden by following the directions below.

Materials:

- a clean jar (A large jelly or peanut butter jar or a small fish bowl works well.)
- ¼ inch (.6 cm) clean pebbles
- damp (but not wet) soil

- fork
- pencil
- tweezers
- small plants

Directions:

Find the Plants ●

Before planting, take a field trip to gather some plants for your gardens. (Small ferns grow well in most environments and are usually easy to find.) When you find a plant, dig carefully around the roots, keeping some soil for protection. Make sure to keep the soil around the roots damp until you plant your garden. (**Note:** Before handling any wild plants, have someone knowledgeable about safe plants to gather help you.)

Prepare the Jar ●

1. Pour the pebbles into the bottle, making a one- to two-inch (2.5–5 cm) layer covering the bottom of the jar. Use your fork to spread the pebbles evenly. The pebbles will make a drainage layer so mud will not become trapped in the bottom of the jar.

2. Pour the soil in on top of the pebbles. You should have about a two- to three-inch (5–8 cm) inch layer of soil in the jar. Use the fork to make a flat surface.

Plant Your Garden ●

Lay your plants out on the table and decide where you will place them in the jar. Use your pencil in the surface of the soil to make small holes that are deep enough for the plant roots. Set the plants into the holes one at a time and use your fork to smooth the soil and to cover the roots. If the opening to your jar is narrow, you may need to use tweezers to help you arrange and adjust your plants properly.

Quiz Time

1. List three major events which take place in this section of the story.

   _____

   _____

   _____

2. How is time split into two parts for the villagers?

   _____

   _____

3. Why do the first two men return to build a house on the beach?

   _____

4. What does Old Gentleman say to the men building on the beach?

   _____

5. Why do you think Jiya wants to return to fishing?

   _____

   _____

6. Why does Kino's father begin to pay Jiya wages for working on the farm?

   _____

   _____

7. What does Kino say when Jiya tells him that he wants to marry Setsu?

   _____

8. What trick does Setsu play on Kino on her wedding day?

   _____

9. Why does Kino begin to feel sad?

   _____

   _____

10. What does Jiya do to prepare for the next big wave?

    _____

    _____

Three-Dimensional Map

In the story *The Big Wave*, Pearl S. Buck incorporates the many land forms of Japan. She writes about a nearby small island, a volcano, narrow sandy beaches, deep pine forests, and a steep hillside that must be terraced so that farmers can plant crops. All of these features can be found throughout the country of Japan.

Work with a partner to make your own three-dimensional map showing the land forms in Japan. Use atlases, resource books, and the information you fill in on the following pages to help shape and design your three-dimensional map.

Materials:

- piece of heavy cardboard
- paint
- stove or hot plate
- pot for mixing dough
- food coloring

Playdough Ingredients:

- 1 cup (250 mL) of flour
- ½ cup (125 mL) salt
- 1 tablespoon (15 mL) oil
- 1 tablespoon (15 mL) cream of tartar
- 1 cup (250 mL) water

Directions:

1. Mix dry ingredients with the oil. Add the water. Cook over medium heat, stirring constantly until dough is stiff. Take dough out of pot and knead until it has the consistency of playdough. (If you want to add food coloring instead of painting the final product, you can color your dough as it is cooking.)

2. Use your dough to spread on the cardboard to form your map. Shape mountains and valleys on the flat surface by molding the dough. You can also add trees, rocks, or other landmarks while the dough is still soft. When it is dry, you can paint the surface to look like your landscape.

3. The dough can be made in advance and packaged in airtight plastic bags for later use.

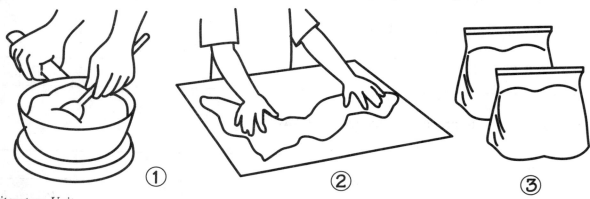

① ② ③

Fear

In the beginning of the story, Jiya is afraid of the sea. While he and Kino are on the small island, Jiya closely watches the ocean for storms. He has learned this fear from his father and the other fishermen in the village who have experienced dangerous storms and waves. At the end of the story, Jiya faces his fear by rebuilding his home on the beach and by making a window to face the sea.

Most people have a slight fear of something, such as spiders, heights, or thunderstorms. These fears are often in response to experiences someone has had in the past, such as walking through a spider web, falling from a loft, or being caught outside in a storm. Although it may seem silly to be afraid of something, fear is very real and facing one's fears can be very difficult.

Think of a few things that you or someone you know are afraid of. List them below. Then brainstorm ideas about what can be done to overcome those fears. When you are finished, choose a partner and take turns role-playing one of the fear scenarios and solutions.

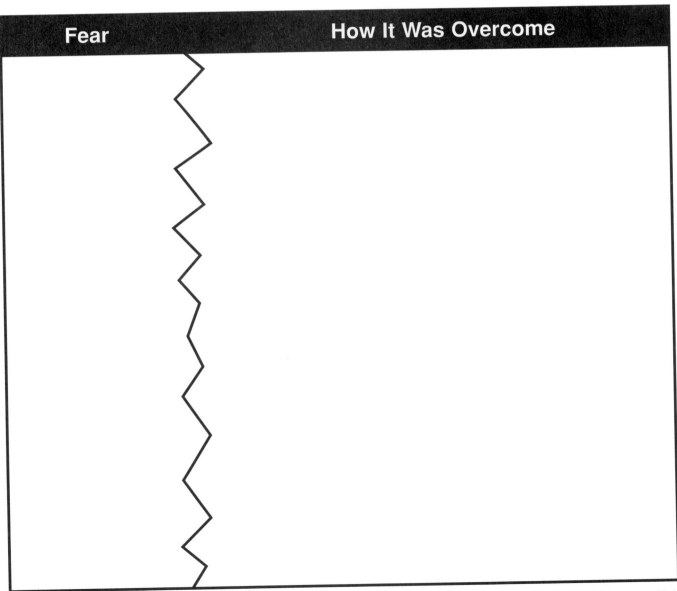

Fear	How It Was Overcome

Japan Map

The country of Japan is actually a series of about 4,000 islands. Mainland Japan consists of the four largest islands. Forested mountains cover most of the land, and there are many active volcanoes throughout these mountains. Japan also has frequent earthquakes because of the volcanoes.

Use books and maps to help you locate and label the cities, landmarks, and features listed on the map below. Use a blue crayon to show water, a green crayon to show flat land, and a brown crayon to show mountains.

Hokkaido
Honshu
Shikoku
Kyushu
Tokyo
Sapporo
Nagasaki
Kyoto
Sea of Japan
Pacific Ocean
Sea of Okhotsk
Japanese Alps
Mt. Fuji

Changes Around Town

As Jiya and Kino grow older, they remember how the fishing village was before the big wave. They remember the fishing huts and the cobbled street. They remember the busy fishermen and their families. One day, as Jiya is looking down the mountain, he sees someone building a house on the sand. Once again there is change on the beach.

Every town changes over time. New houses are built. Old houses are torn down. Schools and stores move, open, and close.

What was your town like when your parents were young?

For this activity you will need to interview a parent (or someone at least your parents' age) who has lived in your town since he or she was a child. Use the questions below to guide your interview. You may want to add some of your own interview questions on the back of this paper. Be prepared to share your information with the class.

Where was your house? _____

Where did you go to school? _____

Where did your family do its grocery shopping? _____

Where did you play? _____

Where did your parents work? _____

Was the main street of town the same as it is now? _____

What used to be where the _____ *is now?*
　　　　　　　　　　　　　　　(fill in the blank with a modern store)

Research Ideas

Describe three things you read in *The Big Wave* that you would like to learn more about.

1. _____

2. _____

3. _____

Pearl S. Buck's story *The Big Wave* is rich with images of landscapes, people, and culture. She writes about personal conflicts and struggles with natural disasters. Further research into these topics will help you to better understand the characters and the story.

Research one or more of the items you named above, or choose one of the ideas listed below. You may work in teams or independently. Be prepared to share the results of your research with your classmates in the form of an oral presentation.

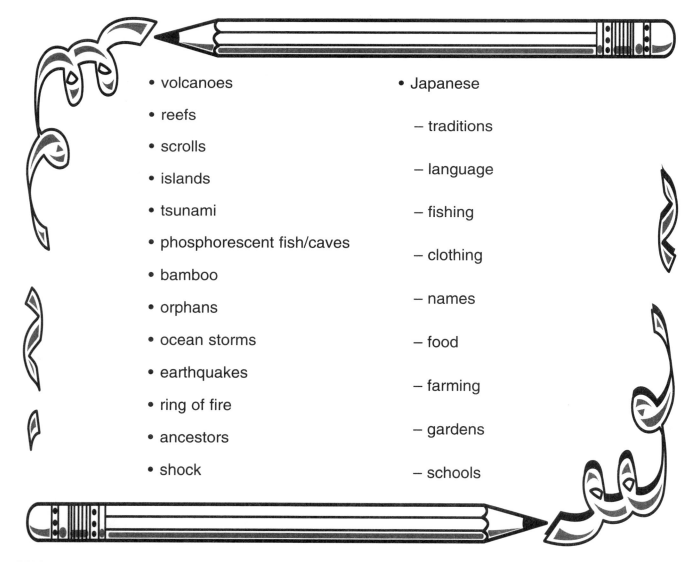

- volcanoes
- reefs
- scrolls
- islands
- tsunami
- phosphorescent fish/caves
- bamboo
- orphans
- ocean storms
- earthquakes
- ring of fire
- ancestors
- shock

- Japanese
  - traditions
  - language
  - fishing
  - clothing
  - names
  - food
  - farming
  - gardens
  - schools

Book Report Ideas

There are many ways to do a book report. After you have finished reading *The Big Wave*, choose one method of reporting that interests you. You may find that although your entire class read the same book, there are a lot of different ideas and opinions about the story to share.

■ Sell It!

Record a two-minute public service announcement or commercial message to sell *The Big Wave* to the public. Include music or background sound effects in your presentation. These additions will make it exciting and attractive to your listeners. Remember that your audience can hear you but not see you.

■ Pen Pal

Write a letter to a character in *The Big Wave*. Tell him or her how different or similar his or her life is from yours. Discuss some of the activities or adventures your character has experienced that you might like to try.

■ Puppet Presentation

Groups of four or five students choose a favorite passage or scene in *The Big Wave*. The groups then design their own puppets and script to present the scene through a puppet play. The individual scenes can be linked together to form a progression of scenes to present the story to another class.

■ Game Time

Create a board game using vocabulary, information, and characters from *The Big Wave*. Display and play the game with classmates.

■ Read All About It!

Write a book review of *The Big Wave* which could be printed in a newspaper. Include the who, what, when, where, and why information from the story. Remember to make your write-up so interesting that the reader will want to read the story.

■ Come and See It!

Design a travel brochure inviting tourists to visit the setting of *The Big Wave*. Include pictures, slogans, characters, and some general information to capture a visitor's attention.

■ Become a Character

This report takes the form of a panel discussion. Each student on the panel adopts the personality of one character in *The Big Wave*. The remaining students may ask the panelists questions about specific scenes in the story or about something totally unrelated, such as what he or she had for breakfast.

■ Character Art

Choose a character to present. Carve a likeness from wood, model from clay, or paint a picture of that character. Write a brief character sketch to accompany your artwork.

■ On the Wall

Design a wall mural as a class. Discuss important scenes from *The Big Wave* and then vote on which of these scenes should be included to tell the story in the mural. Assign groups to work together to create the individual scenes.

Career Day Activities

After Jiya becomes an orphan, he must make choices about where he will live and what career path he will follow. Jiya can become a wealthy scholar or politician if he lives with Old Gentleman. He can continue his life with Kino's family and become a farmer, or he can return to the beach and become a fisherman like his father. Deciding what one will do for a career is both a challenging and an important decision. The following activities will help students explore and learn more about some different career options.

Guest Speakers

Inviting guest speakers to share with your class and to answer questions about their careers is a great way for students to gain firsthand information. It is also a wonderful way to involve parents and friends in the classroom. Choose a week and plan a short time each day for visitors to come in and speak to the class. Send home the letter on page 41 to ask for volunteers. You may also want to plan for a couple of guest speakers of your own in addition to the parent responses that you receive.

Who Wears This Hat?

For this activity, you will need several hats to represent careers. Some ideas might be a nurse's cap, cowboy hat, firefighter's helmet, police officer's cap, football helmet, jockey's helmet, artist's beret, chef's hat, pilot's hat, or a construction worker's hat.

Talk about each hat and who might wear it. Discuss the jobs this person might do and where this person might work. Then ask each student to think about a hat. Have students write a riddle about the person who would wear the hat that they have chosen. For example: I help people in hot places. Sometimes I climb ladders. My clothes are often heavy and wet. Who am I? (Firefighter) Hang the hats around a bulletin board and have students take turns reading their riddles and guessing which hat matches the career. After the contest, display the riddles on the bulletin board for parents and class visitors to read.

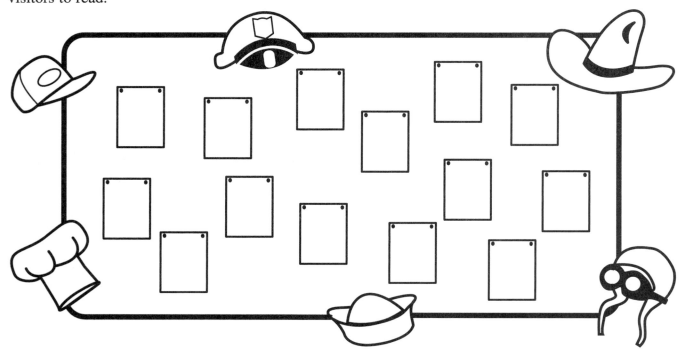

Career Day Activities *(cont.)*

What Do You Like to Do?

Most people choose their careers by thinking about activities that they like to do. For example, someone who likes to draw might be interested in becoming an illustrator. Someone who likes to study science might be interested in becoming a veterinarian. Help students brainstorm job choices by writing subject bubbles on the board. Ask students to think of as many jobs as they can that are related to each subject. Then ask students to think about the subject that they enjoy most and to choose a career under that subject to research. Have students be prepared to present their research information to the class in the form of an oral presentation.

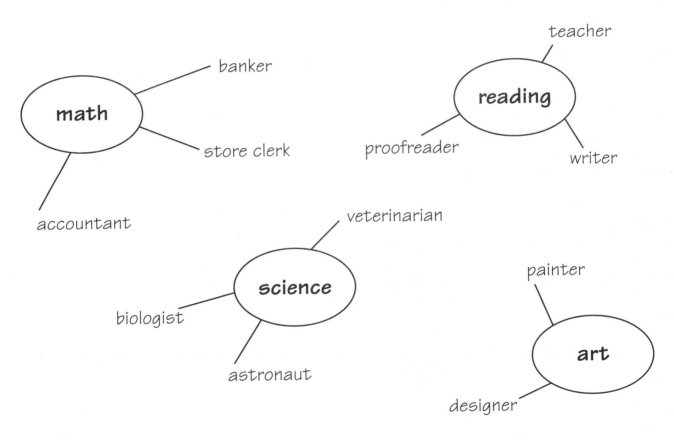

Visit the Workplace

Students can learn much by spending a day in the workplace with an adult. You can arrange to have a day or portion of the day where students accompany their parents or another adult to work. This is a wonderful way for students to see what the workplace is really like and to see what their parents do during the day.

One nationwide program specifically designed for girls to spend a day at work with their mothers or fathers is "Take Our Daughters to Work Day." This program is sponsored by the Ms. Foundation and occurs on the fourth Thursday in April each year. For more information about this program, contact the Ms. Foundation at 1-800-676-7780.

School Subjects and Career Choices

In school you learn about many different subjects. While studying these subjects, you use and improve upon specific skills. For example, in math you learn about numbers, patterns, measuring, computers, sequencing, and problem solving. All of these skills will help prepare you for jobs in the future. Sometimes you may not even think about all of the different skills that you will be using from your school subjects, but every skill you learn may have some future application in a job.

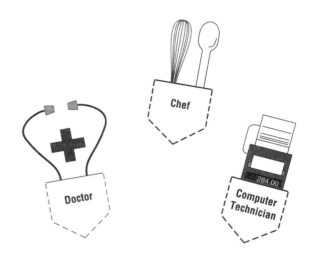

Work with a partner to fill in the chart below. Look at the careers in the first column and then think of what a person doing that career would need to learn from each of the school subjects listed. Write your ideas in the blocks under the subjects. For example, a librarian needs math to help count and sequence books. He or she needs to be able to read in order to know the titles of the books. He or she needs a general knowledge of science topics to be able to direct students to the correct resources for a science project.

Use the blank spaces at the bottom to fill in two career ideas of your own.

Careers	Subjects						
	Writing	Math	Reading	Science	Social Studies	Art	P.E.
Chef							
Accountant							
Computer technician							
Store manager							
Doctor							
Teacher							

Career Days

_____
date

Dear Parents,

As a culminating activity for our unit on *The Big Wave,* we will be holding Career Days in our class. During the week of _____, we will be hosting guest speakers who are interested in sharing their vocations with our class.

If you or a member of your family would be interested in speaking to our class about your career, please notify me by signing and returning the bottom portion of this paper. The students are very excited to share what they have learned and to learn more about some of the jobs in our community. Thank you for your support.

Sincerely,

_____

- -

☐ Yes, I would be interested in sharing my vocation with the class.

_____   _____
name   telephone

_____   _____
child's name   best time to reach me

_____
vocation

Career Day Visitor

Name

Objective Test and Essay

Matching: Match these quotes with the characters who said them by writing the letter from the matching quotation on the line next to the character.

1. _____ Kino's father

2. _____ Old Gentleman

3. _____ Jiya

4. _____ Kino

5. _____ Jiya's father

A. "I knew all the time that I had to come back to the sea."

B. "We must divide ourselves... If the ocean yields to the fires you must live after us."

C. "I have spent my whole life trying to save foolish people from the big wave."

D. "It looks very angry... I shall not sleep tonight."

E. "You would be very foolish to marry Setsu."

True or False: Write true or false next to each statement below.

_____ 6. Jiya is older than Kino.

_____ 7. The fishermen do not fear the sea.

_____ 8. Jiya decides to live with Old Gentleman.

_____ 9. Kino and Jiya attend school in the village.

_____ 10. Jiya becomes a fisherman like his father.

Short Answer: Write a short answer to the following questions.

11. Where do the boys like to play? _____

12. Why is Kino afraid to live in Japan? _____

13. Where did Kino and his family go on vacation last fall? _____

14. Who makes Jiya feel better? _____

15. What happens when the big wave comes? _____

Essay: Write the answers to the following essay topics on the back of this paper.

1. Do you think Jiya should have chosen to live with Old Gentleman? Why or why not?

2. Choose one character from the story whom you would want as a friend. Include in your essay at least three reasons why you think this person would make a good friend.

Response

Identify the speaker and explain the meaning of the following quotes from *The Big Wave*.

Note to the teacher: Choose an appropriate number of quotes for your students to answer.

Section 1   *"The sea is our enemy."*

Section 1   *"You have never been late before, Jiya."*

Section 1   *"I am glad we live on the land... There is nothing to be afraid of on our farm."*

Section 1   *"Look father! The volcano is burning again!"*

Section 2   *"Old Gentleman is telling everyone to be ready... Twice have I seen that flag go up, both times before you were born."*

Section 2   *"I wish Jiya would come. Do you think he will see me if I stand on the edge of the terrace and wave my white girdle cloth?"*

Section 2   *"I have always wanted another son, and Jiya will be that son. As soon as he knows that this is his home, then we must help him to understand what has happened."*

Section 3   *"Yes, we will be happy someday... for life is always stronger than death."*

Section 3   *"Jiya, I will give you my pet duck."*

Section 3   *"I want to go to sleep again."*

Section 3   *"Father, are we not very unfortunate people to live in Japan?"*

Section 4   *"... But I have heard of this boy Jiya and I wish to do more for him. If he is as good as he is handsome, I will make him my own son."*

Section 4   *"I will say,—no!... I thank you but I have a home — on the farm."*

Section 5   *"I want a boat. I want to go back to fishing."*

Section 5   *"You are too silly to be married. I feel sorry for Jiya."*

Section 5   *"I have opened my house to the ocean. If ever the big wave comes back, I shall be ready. I face it. I am not afraid."*

Polar Opposites

Polar opposites are a great way to review a story at the end of a unit. Students gain a deeper understanding of the story through discussion and by defending their opinions. Students also gain the benefit of hearing other viewpoints. (If your students are not familiar with polar opposites, be sure to model a few statements before assigning this sheet.)

Read the statements listed below. Then choose the number ratings closest to the words which you think best complete the statements. Be sure to have examples from the story to support your choices.

1. Kino feels that Japan is a _____ place to live.

    1   2   3   4   5
    safe   **unsafe**

2. Old Gentleman is a _____ man.

    1   2   3   4   5
    generous   **selfish**

3. Kino's and Jiya's families are _____ .

    1   2   3   4   5
    poor   **wealthy**

4. In the story _____ have more important jobs.

    1   2   3   4   5
    fishermen   **farmers**

5. The fishermen _____ the sea.

    1   2   3   4   5
    respect   **disrespect**

6. Jiya is a _____ character.

    1   2   3   4   5
    brave   **cowardly**

7. Jiya made a _____ decision to live with Kino's family.

    1   2   3   4   5
    good   **poor**

8. Jiya is _____ to build his house on the beach after the big wave.

    1   2   3   4   5
    foolish   **wise**

As a follow-up to this sheet, do one or more of the following activities:

1. Get together with a team of three or more students to share your answers. Be prepared to support your choices with examples from the book.

2. Choose one or more of the statements from above and write a paragraph explaining why you chose the number rating. Include examples from the book to support your reasoning.

3. Write some of your own polar opposite statements to accompany the story.

Bibliography of Related Reading

Other Books by Pearl S. Buck

The Beech Tree and Johnny Jack and His Beginnings. (Dell, 1967).

The Big Fight. (John Day, 1965).

The Chinese Children Next Door. (John Day, 1942).

The Chinese Story Teller. (John Day, 1971).

The Christmas Ghost. (John Day, 1960).

Christmas Miniature. (John Day, 1957).

A Gift for the Children. (John Day, 1973).

The Little Fox in the Middle. (Collier Books, 1966).

The Man Who Changed China: The Story of Sun Yet-sen. (Random House, 1953).

Matthew, Mark, Luke, and John. (John Day, 1967).

Mrs. Starling's Problem. (John Day, 1973).

One Bright Day. (John Day, 1950).

Stories for Little Children. (John Day, 1940).

The Water-Buffalo Children and The Dragon Fish. (Dell, 1966).

Welcome Child. (John Day, 1964).

When Fun Begins. (Methuen, 1941).

The Young Revolutionist. (Friendship Press, 1932).

Yu Lan: Flying Boy of China. (John Day, 1945).

Cole, Joanna. *The Magic School Bus® Inside the Earth.* (Scholastic Inc., 1987).

Paul, Aileen. *Kids Gardening.* (Doubleday and Company, Inc., 1972).

Ridgewell, Jenny. *A Taste of Japan.* (Thomas Learning, 1993).

Wells, Ruth. *A To Zen.* (Picture Book Studio, 1992).

Wood, Jenny. *Volcanoes.* (Puffin Books, 1990).

Internet Sites

USA Today Weather @http://www.usatoday.com/weather/wfront.htm

The Weather Channl @http://www.weather.com/

Answer Key

Page 11

1. Accept appropriate events.
2. They are built on terraces and look like steps along the hillside. Most farms have flat fields that are not on the sides of mountains.
3. They live on the beach.
4. He says that the sea is their enemy.
5. Old Gentleman lives in the castle.
6. They feed the sacred deer, collect pebbles, and look for caves.
7. He worries that the ocean god will grow angry.
8. They went to visit a great volcano twenty miles away.
9. The deep, cold, stormy water frightens him.
10. He stays awake to watch the earth and sky for changes.

Page 14

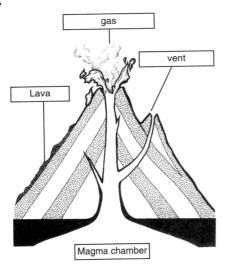

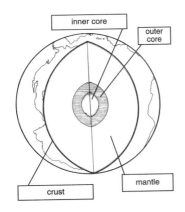

Page 16

1. Accept appropriate events.
2. He raises the flag to tell everyone to be ready for an emergency. He rings the bell to call the people to take shelter with him behind his castle walls.
3. Accept appropriate answers.
4. Accept appropriate answers.
5. He wants to divide his family to be sure that someone will survive if there is a disaster.
6. No. He goes to Kino's farm because he wants to be with his friend's family.
7. It is swept away into the sea.
8. He falls unconscious.
9. Accept appropriate answers such as: Kino needed to release his emotions. Crying is healthy.
10. He says that he will adopt Jiya and that he will become a member of Kino's family.

Page 21

1. Accept appropriate events.
2. They grow calm, quiet, and blue.
3. They kneel beside him and say that he is now a member of their family.
4. She offers to give him her pet duck.
5. Accept appropriate answers such as: He is recovering from shock.
6. He says that life is stronger than death.
7. He does not play but instead works hard beside his father. Answers will vary on part two.
8. He feels happy because the volcano is no longer angry.
9. He is frightened because they live between the volcano and the sea which are both dangerous.
10. He says that to live in danger makes one brave and strong.

Page 26

1. Accept appropriate events.
2. He thinks that Jiya is strong, handsome, intelligent, and the best boy in the village.
3. He plans to give Jiya fine clothes, send him to a good school, and make him a great and honored man.
4. Kino is upset because he does not want to lose his friend.

Answer Key

5. He wants Kino to try to convince his friend to live with Old Gentleman. (He also wants Kino to see the castle so he will understand why Jiya would be better off with Old Gentleman.)

6. Accept appropriate answers such as: The gardener respects Old Gentleman, and Jiya might become his new son.

7. Descriptive examples could include tall, thin, white hair and beard, delicate features, brown smooth skin, proud, wise eyes.

8. Jiya says no, that he has a home on the farm with Kino's family.

9. Accept appropriate answers such as love, friendship, family.

10. Setsu makes Jiya happy and comfortable.

Page 31

1. Accept appropriate events.
2. The times are before and after the wave.
3. They say that the cove has the best fishing, they are tired of having no home, and their fathers lived there before them.
4. He calls them foolish.
5. Accept appropriate answers such as: His heart is with the sea. He wants to do the same job as his father.
6. Jiya wants to buy a boat so he can fish.
7. He says that Jiya is foolish.
8. Setsu hides Kino's brush.
9. He will miss Setsu and Jiya living in the farmhouse.
10. Jiya builds a window facing the sea.

Page 34

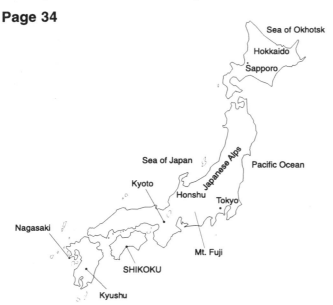

Page 43

Matching

1. D   4. E
2. C   5. B
3. A

True or False

6. True   9. True
7. False   10. True
8. False

Short Answer

11. They play on Old Gentleman's island.
12. He is afraid of volcanoes and the tsunami.
13. They went to the famous great volcano.
14. Setsu makes Jiya feel better.
15. The big wave wipes out the fishing village.

Essay

1. Accept all appropriate answers.
2. Accept appropriate answers supported with details from the story.

Page 44 (in order of section quotes)

1. Jiya
2. Jiya's father
3. Kino
4. Kino
5. Kino's father
6. Kino
7. Kino's father
8. Kino's father
9. Setsu
10. Jiya
11. Kino
12. Old Gentleman
13. Jiya
14. Jiya
15. Kino
16. Jiya

Page 45

Accept appropriate responses supported with examples from the book.